11.93

S0-ALF-118

921
CHA   Roberts, Naurice

        Cesar Chavez and
        La Causa

                        $11.93

921
CHA   Roberts, Naurice

        Cesar Chavez and
        La Causa

                    $11.93

CESAR CHAVEZ and
La Causa

CESAR CHAVEZ and La Causa

by
Naurice Roberts

CHILDRENS PRESS ®
CHICAGO

Picture Acknowledgements:

United Press International—1, 5, 25 (top), 29 (top left and bottom), 31

Photri—2

Archives of Labor and Urban Affairs, Wayne State University—3, 8, 15 (2 photos), 17 (right), 18, 19, 21, 25 (bottom), 26, 27 (right)

AP/Wide World Photos—17 (left) 20, 27 (left), 28, 29 (top right), 30 (left)

United Farm Workers of America/AFL-CIO/Photographs by Victor Aleman—Cover, 6, 9, 11, 13, 22, 23, 30 (right), 32

Library of Congress Cataloging-in-Publication Data

Roberts, Naurice.
  Cesar Chavez and La Causa

  (Picture-stories biographies)
  Summary: Presents an account of the life of the
Mexican American who helped organize farm workers into
a powerful union.
    1. Chavez, Cesar, 1927-   —Juvenile literature.
2. United Farm Workers—Juvenile literature.
3. Migrant agricultural laborers—United States—
Biography—Juvenile literature. [1. Chavez, Cesar,
1927-   . 2. Mexican Americans—Biography.
3. Migrant labor. 4. United Farm Workers—History]
I. Title. II. Series.
HD6509.C48R63 1986   331.88'13'0924 [B] [92] 85-27980
ISBN 0-516-03484-7

CESAR CHAVEZ and
La Causa

Cesar Chavez (at right in checked shirt and sunglasses) led union marches protesting the use of pesticides that endanger the health of migrant workers.

La Causa is Spanish for "The Cause." It is the name given to the workers' movement that was started by Cesar Chavez in 1962.

La Causa led the struggle for human rights and dignity of migrant and farm workers. Within years, the fight, which started in California, spread throughout the United States and the world.

Cesar Chavez understood what it meant to be poor and powerless. He learned this painful lesson when he was a little boy many years ago.

Cesario Estrada Chavez was born March 31, 1927, the oldest son of Librado and Juana Estrada Chavez. He was named for his grandfather, who was called Papa Chayo.

The original Chavez home in Arizona is now deserted.

Papa Chayo had been a slave in Chihuahua, Mexico. Unhappy about the many injustices there, he escaped and crossed the border to the United States in the 1880s.

Papa Chayo settled his family in the Gila Valley near Yuma, Arizona, which was then a territory of the United States.

The family grew quite large. At one time, Cesar counted as many as 180 nieces and nephews. They all lived together on eighty acres of farmland. They raised horses, cows,

In 1982, Librado Chavez celebrated his 100th birthday surrounded by his children and his children's children. His wife, Juana, sits by him hugging one of her great-grandchildren. His son, Cesar, stands next to him.

grain, alfalfa, vegetables, and watermelons. Librado Chavez, Cesar's father, even ran a small country store.

In addition to being storekeeper and farmer, Librado Chavez was also the postmaster because people received mail at the store, too.

Everyone worked hard. Sometimes, Cesar felt his father worked too hard. Everything was going fine, but that would change.

In the 1930s, a dishonest man tricked Librado Chavez in a business deal. Cesar's father lost his land. During this time, the country was in a depression. Millions of people were out of work.

Before long, Mr. Chavez had to sell the store to pay bills. The family then moved into Papa Chayo's old adobe house. It was crowded, but they were all together. Everyone made the best of the situation. Things were very difficult for the family. One day, Cesar's little sister, Helena, became ill. She never got well.

Cesar was always curious. He would ask questions and did everything just like his father did. This was how he learned. He knew how to harness horses and how to water and feed the animals.

The Chavez children, standing behind their parents, Librado and Juana, pose for a birthday portrait. From left to right are Cesar, Ricardo, Vicky, Father Luis Baldomado (the priest who conducted the birthday mass), Rita, and Librado, Jr.

Since there was very little money, people would barter or exchange. In 1933, when sister Eduvigis "Vicky" was born, Mr. Chavez paid the doctor with watermelons.

Times were hard for everyone during the depression. However, the Chavez family was much better off than most. Because they grew their own food they had a little more to eat.

In 1934, Rita, Cesar, Ricardo, and Vicky welcomed a new baby brother. He was named for his father, Librado. The family called him Lenny.

The Chavez children were raised in a very strict home. They always obeyed their parents. Librado and Juana Chavez believed in discipline. But there were plenty of hugs and kisses from Mom and ear tuggings or pats on the head from Dad.

Mrs. Chavez couldn't read or write but she was wise and gave good *consejos*—advice. She taught Cesar about nonviolence. No fighting! He must always turn the other cheek.

She would say, "It takes two to fight. One can't do it alone!"

There were many discussions on

voting rights and citizenship. Mr. Chavez thought it was honorable to stand up for your rights and the rights of others. Cesar thought so, too.

The family was also deeply religious. Cesar's grandmother, Dorotea "Mama Tella," prepared Cesar and Rita for their first communion. Religion would play an even greater role in Cesar's life as he grew older.

Cesar and Helen attend a worker's mass at San Antonio Mission, in California.

Tragedy struck again. The Chavez family lost Papa Chayo's adobe house and ranch because they couldn't pay the back taxes. No one would help. Mr. Chavez couldn't get a loan from the bank. Ten-year-old Cesar thought this was unfair.

The family then joined 300,000 other men, women, and children in California who were migrant workers.

Like the other workers, the Chavez family followed the crops. They went from farm to farm. It was not a good life for anyone. Cesar and his family didn't like it, but there was nothing else to do. They had to earn a living.

The life of a migrant worker was hard. It was not easy to get work. Wages were low and the work in the fields was extremely difficult.

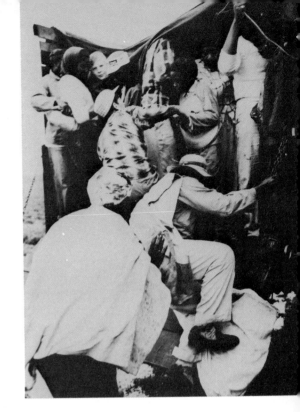

Two families of farm workers shared this tent house (above). Migrant workers—young and old—crowd into trucks (right) that will take them to the fields.

The housing camps, or barrios, were small, cramped, and dirty. There were no bathrooms, sewers, electricity, or running water. And people were not friendly as they had been in Arizona's Gila Valley.

The first year as migrant workers, the family made about $300. It was not much. Cesar soon realized they would probably never see the Gila Valley again.

Things would never be the same
again. Month after month, year
after year, the Chavez family was
on the move. Sometimes twelve
people or more lived in one room.
And there never seemed to be
enough food. Even though the
family didn't have much, they
always shared with others.

Some of the farm workers'
children went to school. Cesar
went, too, but didn't like it. Some
teachers weren't always nice to him.
He couldn't speak English very
well. Big sister Rita would help. She
was the smart one. Altogether, the
Chavez children attended over thirty
different schools.

Cesar and his brother Ricardo
teamed up to help out. Not only
did they work in the fields, but they

Migrant workers, such as the grape picker (left) and the tomato picker (right), received low wages. For example, if a worker was lucky enough to work for a full year, the worker might earn $6,000. But finding full-time work was rare. In the mid-1970s most migrant workers earned only about $2,500 in a year.

found all kinds of odd jobs to make extra money for food. When they could, they swept floors at the theater so they could see the Lone Ranger movies.

Cesar was fifteen when he graduated from eighth grade in 1942. Graduation was a great achievement for Cesar. Most children of migrant workers never went beyond the sixth grade.

The years passed. In 1942, Cesar graduated from eighth grade. Instead of going on to high school, he decided to work in the fields full time. The family really needed him. Besides, his parents were getting older and farm work was especially hard on them.

Many farm workers would argue over wages. Some growers or labor contractors were mean and tried to cheat the migrants. If other workers quit, the Chavez family would do the same.

By this time, 1944, World War II was on and Cesar joined the navy. At seventeen, he just wanted to get away from everything. After the war, Cesar was glad to get back home. He was happy to see his family and Helen, a girl he had met several years earlier.

In 1948, Ricardo married. Later Rita and then Cesar married, too. Soon, Cesar Chavez had a family of his own.

Helen and Cesar and their children

Cesar spoke to farm workers at a ceremony honoring a worker who was killed on a picket line. The workers' strike for better pay and better working conditions was long and hard. Some workers died for La Causa.

Now more than ever Cesar wanted to do something to help his people. Conditions for the migrant workers had not improved. In fact, they were getting worse.

Cesar began meeting and talking with other angry farm workers. He found out that they had the same ideas and feelings. Cesar read books and learned about the law. He knew that many things the owners did to farm workers were illegal.

He started working with the Community Service Organization. The CSO helped farm workers and other poor people. There Cesar was able to help people get food, better housing, medical care, and legal aid. The work was very rewarding.

The CSO also helped people register to vote. Voting was real power. Cesar began organizing. Some people thought Mexican-Americans shouldn't be able to vote. But this was a right of all citizens. It didn't matter where a person was born.

A worker signs up to fight for his right to vote and to earn a living wage.

Farm workers used peaceful marches to gain support for their cause.

The migrant farm workers and their supporters got together and marched, too. They marched for dignity, justice, and human rights. Many times they sang Mexican songs or yelled slogans.

"We want jobs! We want jobs!" they shouted.

Jobs were very important to everyone. Jobs meant greater wages and a better life. Cesar looked around at the marchers. "The farm workers really needed a union," he thought.

On September 30, 1962, the National Farm Workers Association was founded in Fresno, California. La Causa was born. Cesar quit the CSO to work with the union. He did this without pay. Money was not important.

Cesar went from farm to farm talking with workers. The entire Chavez family helped. Some

workers were afraid to join the union. They thought the big growers would be angry and they would lose their jobs. It was a struggle, but Cesar convinced them to join. The union grew.

"*Huelga! Huelga!*" was the farm workers' cry. *Huelga* means strike. Unless pay and working conditions got better, no one would work in the fields. Without the migrant workers, crops rotted in the fields. This made the growers very angry. There were fights and beatings. But still no one worked.

There were a few victories. However, they were hard fought. Some union members even went to jail. Then Chavez and the union called for a boycott. They asked people not to buy grapes or lettuce.

Cesar (above) held rallys in Boston, Massachusetts and other major cities throughout the United States. Although these cities were a long way from the picket lines (below) in California, Cesar wanted all Americans to support the migrant workers by refusing to buy any product not picked by union pickers.

Helen Chavez and Robert Kennedy were with Cesar the day he broke his 25-day fast. Cesar's fast was his nonviolent way of bringing attention to the problems and poverty of the migrant worker in America.

Robert Kennedy believed in Cesar Chavez and La Causa. He supported the boycott. So did Dr. Martin Luther King, Jr. Although the union leader never met Dr. King, he talked to him by telephone. Cesar liked what the civil rights leader was doing to help blacks fight for their rights.

The United Farm Workers (UFW) calls for a new boycott against grape growers who refuse to sign union contracts.

In 1974, Cesar Chavez and Bishop Joseph Donnelly met with Pope Paul VI (right) in Rome.

After a number of years the union's name was changed to the United Farm Workers.

In 1974, Cesar Chavez went to Europe to talk about the boycott. He talked with union officials and even with the pope. All gave their support to La Causa.

27

An exhausted Cesar, fighting fatigue and hunger, speaks to striking farm workers. At the time this photo was taken, Cesar was on the fifth day of a water-only fast and a 70-mile walk for La Causa.

Back home, the struggle continued with more boycotts and picketing. There was also violence and threats to Cesar's life and the lives of other union workers. They all refused to quit. They would not be stopped!

The union didn't believe in violence. Instead they would march and pray. Cesar had great faith.

Led by Cesar Chavez, the United Farm Workers used marches, boycotts, strikes, and rallys to gain financial and political support for their cause.

The Chavez family from left to right: Paul, Ana, Anthony, Linda, Fernando, Helen, Eloise, Cesar, Sylvia, and Linda. Each member fights for the rights of migrant workers.

In 1985, Cesar and his nine-year-old granddaughter, Monica Delga led several hundred UFW workers on a ten-mile march to protest California Governor George Deukmejian's farm labor policies.

Sometimes he would fast, going without food for a long time. He did everything he could to get support for La Causa.

Now, more and more people are involved—even Cesar's children and grandchildren. There has been great public support for the boycotts all across the country. Marches and demonstrations continue to be the weapons Cesar uses to get better wages and living conditions for migrant workers.

These young Chicanos were part of a larger group that marched 600 miles from Calexico to Sacramento, California to protest discrimination against Americans of Mexican descent.

Today, Cesar Chavez is still the father of La Causa. He believes in the dignity, justice, and human rights of all people, especially the poor. Only when people come together can they have power and improve their lives.

For Cesar Chavez this is the greatest cause of all.

CESAR CHAVEZ

1927	March 31—Cesario Estrada Chavez born near Yuma, Arizona
1937	Librado Chavez loses the farm. The Chavez family become migrant workers in California
1942	Cesar graduates from eighth grade and works in the fields full time
1944	Cesar joins the navy and fights in World War II
1948	Cesar marries
1950s	Cesar quietly begins to study and work for better working conditions for migrant workers. Later he joins Community Service Organization (CSO)
1962	September 30—the National Farm Workers Association is founded in Fresno, California. La Causa begins
1965	Workers' strike begins against California grape growers
1970	Chavez calls for nationwide boycott of lettuce; the grape boycott ends
1973	Union renamed the United Farm Workers of America (UFW); boycott grape growers begins again
1978	Boycotts against grape and lettuce growers ends
1985	Union farm workers march for better wages and better working conditions

ABOUT THE AUTHOR

NAURICE ROBERTS has written numerous stories and poems for children. Her background includes work as a copywriter, television personality, commercial announcer, college instructor, communications consultant, and human resources trainer. She received a B.A. in Broadcast Communications from Columbia College in Chicago where she presently resides. Her hobbies include working with young people, lecturing, and jogging. She has written books about Andrew Young, Barbara Jordan, and Henry Cisneros.